Psychiatric Rights (Rites?)

Psychiatric Rights (Rites?)

✦

A Treatise on Involuntary Mental Hospitalization and Thomas Szasz

by Mark Vellucci, M.A.

iUniverse, Inc.
New York Lincoln Shanghai

Psychiatric Rights (Rites?)
A Treatise on Involuntary Mental Hospitalization and Thomas Szasz

All Rights Reserved © 2004 by Mark Anthony Vellucci

No part of this book may be reproduced or transmitted in any form or by any means, graphic, electronic, or mechanical, including photocopying, recording, taping, or by any information storage retrieval system, without the written permission of the publisher.

iUniverse, Inc.

For information address:
iUniverse, Inc.
2021 Pine Lake Road, Suite 100
Lincoln, NE 68512
www.iuniverse.com

ISBN: 0-595-31272-1

Printed in the United States of America

Contents

Introduction 1

CHAPTER 1   General Description of the Work of
Thomas Szasz 3

CHAPTER 2   An Analysis and Discussion of Thomas Szasz'
Psychiatric Slavery 13

CHAPTER 3   Autonomous Psychotherapy and the Ethics of
Involuntary Mental Hospitalization 21

CHAPTER 4   The Adversarial Position of the Mentally Ill in
Society 25

CHAPTER 5   Integration of Theories and Issues 33

CHAPTER 6   Responsibility of the Community at Large 47

CHAPTER 7   "Medicine and the State: A Humanist
Interview" 55

CHAPTER 8   Mental Illness—A Debate Between Dr. Albert
Ellis and Dr. Thomas Szasz 61

Suggestions for Further Reading/Information 71

Introduction

The issue of involuntary mental hospitalization is one that has created a great deal of controversy among psychiatrists, psychologists, sociologists, criminal studies experts, and other social scientists. While there seem to be many justifications for committing those designated as "insane" to a psychiatric hospital, further study and exploration raises many serious questions about the validity of the entire process. This method of incarceration has been brought under serious scrutiny in recent times. There are, in fact, proposals to completely eliminate it, as raised by prominent scholars in the field. Among these advocates is included Dr. Thomas Szasz, whose work will be of primary focus.

Whether or not involuntary mental hospitalization should exist is quite a broadly phrased question, and one which needs to be refined and placed into context. While it is true that Dr. Szasz and many of his proponents support the abolition of involuntary mental hospitalization, their arguments are generally referring to those whose commitment has been strictly based on legally designated non-criminal behavior. The issue is strongly grounded in a discussion of civil liberties, law, and criminal justice. The medicalization of mental disorders, providing the context for allowing the establishment and continuation of involuntary mental hospitalization, is a factor, which will also be investigated.

This work is intended to present a highly controversial point of view in such a manner as to raise serious doubts about the effectiveness of a mental hospitalization system that includes involuntary incarceration as one of its elements. Whether or not involuntary mental hospitalization should be abolished is often viewed very differently by reasonable, well-intentioned individuals working in the mental health profession. The issue of involuntary mental hospitalization is of social and political concern for all members of society. There is sometimes a fine line in determining who is or is not a candidate for involuntary mental hospitalization. It is the responsibility of all citizens to see to it that our civil rights come first in the decision-making process.

1

General Description of the Work of Thomas Szasz

The work of Thomas Szasz tends to evoke very strong, although not always positive reactions. His sharp-tongued, attacking style is poorly received in the traditional psychiatric and psychological community, where his ideas are considered to be quite radical. In order to understand his ideas clearly, it is necessary to be introduced to the fundamental underpinnings of his work. In this chapter, I will provide the foundations of the theories of Thomas Szasz, from which his theories on the abolition of involuntary mental hospitalization have been developed.

Thomas Szasz first began publishing his works in 1947 (Vatz & Weinberg, 1983). Although initially publishing articles dealing with physical manifestations of psychiatric disorders, e.g. "The Role of Hostility in the Pathogenesis of Peptic Ulcer…" (1947) and "Psychosomatic Research" (1953), by the mid-1950s he was beginning to move his work more toward a questioning of established psychological principles, e.g. "Malingering: 'Diagnosis' or Social Condemnation…" (1956). Since that time he has produced numerous works on the subject of mental illness and his primary contention that mental illness is not a disease (see suggestions for further reading). While this idea is viewed as preposterous by many, Szasz has made his case in a systematic, logical manner. This work had led to many reforms in the structure of mental hospitals (Vatz, et al.), and has led to an increased awareness of the rights of the individual, whether labeled mentally ill or not.

This review of Szasz's major contentions and primary concepts, to be sure, will not be an exhaustive discussion, but rather a brief survey from which to proceed with a detailed analysis of the process of mental hospitalization in society today. It would be quite conceivable to produce a lengthy analysis on any one of the primary contentions introduced in this section. I will, however, present material I believe is most fundamental to an understanding of Szasz's position on involuntary mental hospitalization.

The introduction of the following concepts will provide a frame of reference in which Szasz's work might be more clearly understood. Szasz's work in involuntary mental hospitalization is predicated on the idea that in a free society no person should be deprived of his or her civil liberties without due process of law. To incarcerate a person when no crime has been committed is a violation of civil liberties which requires reform.

Mental Illness is Not a Disease

A primary contention of Thomas Szasz's work is that mental illness is not a disease (Szasz, 1974). He believes that mental illness does not share the common characteristics of a traditionally defined disease. Mental illness cannot be isolated to a particular part of the body and tangibly identified as such. "If a brain lesion or chemical imbalance could be discovered, for example, then we would no longer have a mental illness, but rather a physiological one" (Szasz, 1977, cassette tape). Szasz also contends that a mental illness is the only type of "disease" which cannot be present in a corpse (Szasz & Ellis, 1977). A cancer, for example, is present whether or not a person is dead, but is psychosis? Perhaps if it had a physiological manifestation, but then it would not be a mental illness, it would be a physiological one:

> "It is possible, indeed it is likely, that there are brain diseases as yet undiscovered by medical science. But that fact has no bearing on what is conventionally considered to be the problem of mental illness" (Szasz, 1973, p.9).

If mental illness does not meet the criteria for being a disease, then what do we call all of the "crazy" behavior we see just about every day in various forms? For Szasz, it is not a question of a person's actions seeming crazy to himself, but of his or her disturbing behavior as perceived by those around him. If a person is disturbing to others and behaving criminally, then Szasz feels this is within the realm of the criminal justice system, not the psychiatric profession (1977, p.117). By the same token, if a person is disturbing in some ways but has not engaged in any criminal activity, then that person needs to be left to his own devices in a free society (Szasz, 1974). The state-run mental hospitals under our current system are given the authority to imprison and "treat" those individuals who have committed no crime, but have acted in a disturbing manner and have been identified as having done so by a person given license to make that determination. For Szasz, "crazy" behavior is nothing more than a description of that behavior which most of society does not approve:

> "What is considered illness or insanity is, generally, simply an arbitrary determination" (1977, p.53).

Personal Autonomy

The concept of personal autonomy is critical to an understanding of Thomas Szasz's work. Although a psychiatrist, Szasz is also a man who is keenly interested in philosophy, sociology, and law. His particular conceptualization of personal autonomy is that individuals should have the freedom to behave as they please and to make decisions as they see fit, so long as they do not violate the law (Szasz, 1974). This concept must be adhered to in a free society. There are many restrictions placed on individuals in a complex society, such as the inability to purchase some medications without a prescription (Szasz, 1977), the infiltration of American communist or socialist organizations by government agents, and the commitment of those deemed as mentally ill to incarceration in a mental hospital based solely on psychiatric recommendation. While it is essential that society be protected and regulated for purposes of protection, this duty should not be made a responsibility of the psychiatric profession, as is often the case (Szasz, 1983).

Personal autonomy is a concept that cannot be effectively put into practice without its corollary, personal responsibility. While it is desirable for people to be able to make choices and exercise their rights in a free society, these ideals cannot be achieved without a clearly defined sense of social and personal responsibility. This sense of accountability to one's fellow citizens is based on commonly held moral and ethical principles which are the fabric of a well-functioning society. Laws and regulations are not, in themselves, enough to maintain a society of autonomous individuals. The ability of members of a community to practice their lifestyle as they so desire needs to be tempered by their willingness to participate in that community. If individuals choose to be personally autonomous regardless of their impact on their community, they may remove themselves from that group. There is the option to pursue one's lifestyle in a free society, but there is also a corresponding obligation to be aware of the social values and ethics prevalent in that society.

Thomas Szasz believes that as long as a person can be committed to a mental institution against his will, although committing no crime, then we all are within a psychiatrist's statement of being put in the same predicament (p.56). Personal autonomy begins when people are allowed to express themselves freely, without fear of government reprisal (1974):

> "I think we should think of it [personal autonomy] more as the right to disagree with and reject authority…and of course the right

to take one's chances with one's own judgment and decision" (1977, p.162).

Language as Power

An important concept in Szasz's theories is that of the use of language as a way of securing power in the psychiatric profession (1974). Szasz contends that by using scientific-type definitions for psychiatric illnesses, the profession creates the misimpression that it is a science, in much the same way as is chemistry or astronomy (1974). To couch theory in scientific language has added credibility to the social sciences, but it has also created unrealistic expectations. Human behavior, while sometimes generally classifiable, does not easily fit into neatly packaged scientific formulations. Szasz believes that the use of scientific language by psychiatrists and psychologists "is a method by which these disciplines may achieve higher regard and, as a consequence, greater power in society" (1977, p.160). This has indeed proven to be the case in our current judicial system, where the testimony of psychiatrists and psychologists is often requested by a court, and is regarded in much the same light as any other "expert" testimony. Szasz feels that most social research is actually *scientistic* in nature—"it (social research) is a fraudulent attempt at duplicating scientific procedures" (Szasz & Ellis, 1977, cassette tape).

Language may also be a very powerful mechanism when used in the description of the mentally ill. Many times throughout Szasz's work he points to the use of language as a way of justifying the current system of treatment of the "mentally ill." By referring to involuntary commitments as forms of "patient interventions," and by continually utilizing the language of helplessness ("they can't help themselves," "we just want to help those poor people," "they need our help," etc.), the practice of involuntary mental hospitalization has become an acceptable form of treatment in the public's view. The concept of the benevolent doctor and the poor, helpless patient is widely accepted by many in our society, including civil libertarians and humanists, who under most other circumstances would surely be up in arms. The terminology of the "doctor" and the "patient," as administrator of therapy and as recipient of such therapeutic intervention respectively, when applied to mental illness, places the identified mentally ill person in a vulnerable position (1987, p.324).

Another aspect of language as power is the use of the language of intervention. The doctor is often referred to as the "therapist' when treating the mentally ill, so therefore it follows logically that the patient (client) will be receiving therapy or treatment and is, therefore, "ill." This, I believe, is crucial, because it affords the doctor the opportunity to practice almost any intervention he so chooses, so long as he calls it therapy. This may include less intrusive therapies such as talk therapy, but might also include electroshock, lobotomy, etc., and may be performed with or without the involuntary patient's permission. Language, and the institutions society designates and empowers, become the key ingredients in these situations. Without the language as such, many interventions might not be justifiable, but the use of language colors the perception of the situation and creates an appearance of complete propriety in a system compatible with a generalized interpretation of personal autonomy, care, illness, and responsibility.

Humanism

Szasz believes in "the affirmation of the individual against the group, the layman against the expert" (1977, p.162), and sees humanism as much a political concept as a philosophical, ethical, or psychological one. In Szasz's view, as expressed by Dr. Paul Kurtz and confirmed by Szasz, humanism "draws deeply from the well of freedom—freedom of the individual—and considers it to be its central value" (1977, p.161). It is a concept that may be approached from "two entirely different ways," as Szasz explains:

> "One is by trying to define the good life, the good person—tolerance, openness, love, reason, whatever the definer values. The artic-

ulation and realization of that kind of life...becomes humanism. The other approach...is to say instead—and this is the view I prefer, that humanism is the result, the consequence of an optimal or maximal pluralism and diversity in society" (p. 161)

Humanism, in the second approach articulated by Szasz, is not a particular way of living, but is rather the complex and rich diversity that is the result of people being allowed to live their lives as they so choose. Humanism, in this context, maximizes personal autonomy and freedom of choice, and "has no meaning outside a political and socioeconomic context that provides and protects the range of choices available" (p. 161). Humanism goes well beyond the scope of psychology. It is a "unification of personality, training, and conviction," and "a certain unification of temperament, intellect, and ethics" (Erickson, 1964, p. 237) that characterizes humanistic thought and behavior.

In the humanist perspective espoused by Szasz, freedom for the individual and a free society are equally essential elements. Humanism, though most often expressed in ethical and psychological terms, is also a political concept. The "one notion" that Szasz chooses to emphasize in the politics of humanism is dissent:

> "After all, authorities never object to people agreeing with them. But they get unhappy and often quite nasty when people disagree with them. So it's disagreement that must be nurtured and protected" (p. 162).

The preservation of dissent, while a readily acceptable ideal in the context of American society, requires a commitment that is lacking in current-day political reality. A return to humanist principles in politics would open the door to "unexplored promises and possibilities" (p. 162).

The concept of humanism which Szasz espouses is vital to the understanding of the perspective from which he writes. The opportunity for the individual to achieve personal autonomy is a humanistic goal for Szasz, and is very much a part of his opposition to control by authorities. Szasz feels that the "therapeutic state" (1970, p.75) is the most threatening element to his concept of humanism because it allies medicine and the state in a powerful way. Any excessive concentration of power is a threat to a truly free society. Szasz sees the therapeutic state as being dangerously powerful:

> "whereas child and madman lack the power to impose their role playing on unconsenting others, psychiatrists, invested with the coercive power of the state, often impose their definitions of reality on others. Hence, in the therapeutic state, care, help, and treatment are not what the involuntary patients request, but what the humanitarian psychiatrists impose" (1970, p.91).

The preceding discussion has established a framework upon which to expand the concepts of Thomas Szasz. As will be shown, the Szaszian perspective on involuntary mental hospitalization is founded upon the concepts of humanism, personal autonomy, and the contention that mental illness is not a disease. The issues presented in this chapter will be elaborated and expanded upon throughout this work. The following chapters will build upon issues presented heretofore, with primary emphasis given to the rights of the individual in a free society, and the ways in which those rights are threatened by the "rites" called psychiatry, psychology, and psychotherapy.

References

Erickson, Erik H. (1964). *Insight and Responsibility.* Toronto, CA: George J. McLeod Limited.

Szasz, Thomas. (1970). *Justice in the Therapeutic State.* In *The Administration of Justice in America: The 1968-69 E. Paul du Pont Lectures on Crime, Delinquency, and Corrections (75-92).* Newark, DL: University of Delaware Press.

Szasz, Thomas. (1974). *Ceremonial Chemistry: The Ritual Persecution of Drugs, Addicts, and Pushers.* New York: Doubleday.

Szasz, Thomas. (1977). *Psychiatric Slavery.* New York: The Free Press.

Szasz, Thomas. (1977). *The Theology of Medicine.* Baton Rouge, LA: LSU Press.

Szasz, Thomas S. & Ellis, Albert (Speakers). (1977). *Mental Illness: Fact or Myth* (Cassette Tape). Baldwin, N.Y.: W.E. Simon.

Vatz, Richard E. & Weinberg, Lee S. (Eds.) (1983). *Thomas Szasz: Primary Values and Major Contentions.* Buffalo, N.Y.: Prometheus Books.

2

An Analysis and Discussion of Thomas Szasz' <u>Psychiatric Slavery</u>

The notion of imprisoning a person without due process is one which our society generally finds unacceptable. Yet, contends Dr. Thomas Szasz in his book entitled *Psychiatric Slavery,* the institutionalization of mental patients is very often nothing more than a form of imprisonment without the processes we as American citizens have a right to demand. It is this social hypocrisy that Szasz objects to and, using the legal case of Donaldson v. O'Connor, seeks to expose.

If *Psychiatric Slavery* might be boiled down to one basic premise, it would be that it is a form of imprisonment to keep people against their will in a mental institution. Szasz believes that individuals have the right to <u>refuse</u> treatment as well as to demand it, depending on the wants of that person (p. 9). Quite often mental patients are forced to undergo various "treatments" administered by a hospital psychiatrist whose conduct "as judged by the recipients of his benevolence, is deemed to be not treatment, but torture, with consequences again being all too familiar" (p. 10). Namely, consequences such as impairment of brain functioning through repeated electroshock administrations, unwanted or unnecessary prescription drug interventions, or continued incarceration against one's wishes. Szasz believes in the abolition of involuntary hospitalization, and argues effectively for that position throughout the book.

The case referred to earlier, that of Donaldson v. O'Connor, presented a fertile ground on which to develop the support for abolition of involuntary hospitalization. Donaldson had been committed to an institution by his parents even though he had steadfastly maintained that he did not require hospitalization. O'Connor was his psychiatrist in the state hospital. The case centered on Donaldson's contention that O'Connor had not given him treatments while in the hospital, even though he had personally sought court injunctions to stop several treatments based on his Christian Scientist religion. The case involved a number of complex issues, such as (1) does a patient have a right to demand treatment, (2) can a state-employed psychiatrist be held liable if he is following the rules of the state and other court-imposed restrictions, (3) does a patient have a right to refuse treatment, then hold his doctors accountable for not treating him, and (4) can or should a person be in a mental hospital and receive no treatment?

All of these issues, however, are overshadowed, according to Szasz, by the question of whether or not mental institutions should exist with policies of involuntary commitment. Szasz feels that everyone involved with the Donaldson v. O'Connor case missed the point—they were attempting to improve a system which, by that very attempt, has its existence justified (p. 38). He feels that this case, instead of centering on whether or not Donaldson had a right to treatment, should have focused on how it is that people in a free society could be forced to be hospitalized against their will.

Major Contentions On Involuntary Institutionalization

It is the view of Thomas Szasz that ultimately all citizens not convicted of a crime have a right to make choices (p. 53). To separate a classification of people from the rest of society and not afford them the same rights as others is clearly contradictory to our societal beliefs. Why is it, then, that we allow the involuntary commitment of mental patients?

To a great extent, believes Szasz, it is out of a misguided sense of compassion and paternalism promulgated by the psychiatric profession (p. 53). The state acts as the agent to this psychiatric fraud by permitting incarceration by "paternalistic figures" who want to "help those who can't help themselves" (p. 53). This notion, says Szasz, can be summed up as follows: "the public-interest psychiatrists assume the role of 'doctor knows best'; the public-interest lawyers, that of 'attorney knows best'" (p. 53).

People need to be able to decide for themselves whether or not they desire treatment. There is no so-called "right to treatment," as has been argued by the American Civil Liberties Union, any more than there is a right to treatment of persons with a physical illness. To argue for a right to treatment presupposes that a psychiatrist is able to determine who actually does and does not need treatment. The psychiatrist often claims to know that a person "needs" treatment even if he insists that he is well; again, doctor knows best. To allow that kind of power to be wielded by the state places all citizens in jeopardy of losing their freedom at the discretion of the psychiatric profession.

By arguing for a "right to treatment," civil liberties groups actually legitimize the process of involuntary incarceration. The argument should instead be for a complete abolition of state-run mental institutions. To argue for improvement of a system is acknowledging that it should exist (p. 90). To establish the goal of reforming state institutions and replacing them with more humane facilities, such as clinics, would entrench the practice of involuntary commitment further (p. 90). The true civil libertarian position would be to call for equal treatment under the law of all people not convicted of crimes. No more, no less.

One argument that is often presented by the psychiatric community is that mentally ill people frequently do not realize their condition, and thus sometimes need to be "saved from themselves." Szasz discusses this point at length, beginning with his definition of the religion of psychology: "mental illness is an illness that requires treatment especially when the patient has no insight into the need for it" (p. 38). This presents quite a paradox—how can someone know something about another person's mind that he himself has no knowledge of? Earlier in the book, Szasz discusses the psychiatrists' view of schizophrenia. He says:

> "The cardinal characteristics of paranoid schizophrenia are, first, that the patient makes claims about himself or the world with which psychiatrists and the society they represent disagree; and second, that the patient insists that he is normal or sane, whereas the psychiatrists and the society they represent insist that he is crazy or insane" (p. 22).

These points raise many questions about the dependence on subjective measures as a means to determine that people should be incarcerated against their will.

Szasz believes that our society has become overly accepting and unquestioning of psychiatric tenets. Psychiatric terms and diagnoses define conflict out of existence. There can be no questioning of diagnoses and descriptions once they are defined. Once defined, they are; they exist, no questions. By resolving conflict through definition, the psychiatric profession has produced an impressive "dictionary" of mental disorders (*Diagnostic and Statistical Manual*). Our society generally accepts the diagnoses of psychiatrists as being equally valid to those of a physician, due in large measure to psychiatry's having opted to define disorders as though they had indisputable manifestations (Szasz, 1977).

Another fallacy sometimes presented as support for the involuntary institutionalization of mental patients is the idea that if people can be treated and improved or cured, then hospitalization against their will is a good idea. Szasz feels that this is merely a case of the ends justifying the means; the so-called aims of treatments or actions cannot be justified based on their perceived curative ability (p. 112). Additionally, the patient is placed in a very self-incriminating position when confronted by institutional psychiatrists. If a person is unwilling to be institutionalized and realizes that if he is honest he will be incarcerated, an acucurate diagnosis of him cannot be made. It would clearly be in the prospective patient's self-interest to say whatever the doctors seem to want to hear (p. 123).

If there is a "right to treatment," it seems to be in conflict with the right against self-incrimination (p 123). To demand treatment is to admit a grounds for having one's freedoms taken from him. A clear conflict also arises in the role of the psychiatrist—as agent of the state he is required to report on his patients' conditions, which will often result in a conflict between the psychiatrist's loyalty to his patient and to the state. In this context, it seems clear that a truly therapeutic relationship can never exist between psychiatrist and patient. The psychiatrist is essentially a warden over his prisoners. Such conflict cannot be eliminated until involuntary hospitalization is abolished.

Ramifications of Advocating Abolition of Involuntary Hospitalization

What is the goal of involuntary mental hospitalization? Supposedly it is to restore the mentally ill to a state of mental health in which they will be able to function in society. In reality, many people, once admitted, will never be released, regardless of their wishes or desires. However, many patients realize that if they "confess by word or act of faith" (p. 112), they may be on the road to freedom. If they can fit into some socially prescribed norm of "reality," they stand an excellent chance of being labeled "well." "Therein, precisely," according to Szasz, "lies the tragedy of psychiatric slavery" (p. 112). It is a system based on deception, that of psychiatrist with patient, and vice versa. It is an unworkable conflict of interest for a psychiatrist to be both an agent of an incarceratory state system and of a patient.

With all of the preceding points articulated, several questions arise, not the least of which is why some in the psychiatric profession endorse the continuation of the practice of incarcerating "mental patients" against their will? Additionally, why does the psychiatric profession not demand change and refuse to participate in such practices? According to Szasz, "there is nothing clinical about psychiatric prisons and imprisonment. To view loss of liberty under psychiatric auspices from a clinical perspective is to endorse it" (p. 56). The American Psychiatric Association has been arguing for improvements in the current system, which again legitimizes the concept of institutionalization. The question of improving the system is of no real consequence to many of the arguments Szasz presents, except in that the question points to the need for psychiatrists to realize the damage this system is causing and the ultimate need for its abolition. Szasz does contend that psychiatrists could at least have improved conditions had they chosen, saying "…a psychiatrist…need not be a psychiatric slave master" (p. 73). The APA blames a lack of funding for the poor conditions in hospitals and says that state hospitals are not equipped to handle certain types of patients even though they continue to admit them (p. 73). They missed the point that while it would be preferable to improve conditions for currently enrolled patients, the ultimate objective should be to eliminate involuntary institutionalization completely.

Another effect of psychiatry is in the judicial system, specifically in regard to a person's legal rights. It is quite a real possibility that a person can be deprived of his legal right to a trial or hearing if that person is defined as "mentally ill." There are numerous accounts of people being found mentally incompetent to stand trial and involuntarily committed to a state institution. The irony here is that many civil liberties groups see the insanity defense as a humane way for society to treat its "mentally ill," when in reality a person may be deprived of many of his civil liberties (right to trial, right against self incrimination, rights of due process) if a psychiatrist pronounces him mentally unfit. People who thus may have been found innocent of a crime are instead sent off for "treatment," having been denied the right to trial (p. 117).

In Summation

Dr. Szasz argues with great zeal in *Psychiatric Slavery* for the abolition of all involuntary commitment to mental institutions. He believes that there are fundamental flaws in the current structure, including (1) conflicts of interest between the state, psychiatrists, and so-called psychiatric patients, (2) a removal of basic rights and civil liberties from an arbitrarily defined group of people, (3) a concentration of power in the hands of the psychiatric profession, and (4) the failure to actually provide any proven method of identifying and treating mental hospital patients. The current system is so fundamentally flawed it is not worthy of adjustment, but should instead be abolished.

The current system places a great deal of reliance on a field in which there is a tremendous divergence of opinion. There is an inherent danger in this—that of elevating the field of psychiatry to a status where its foundations may not be questioned. By allowing psychiatry to occupy a position of such immense power, we legitimize its status and accept its attempt to define itself as an unquestioned, wholly accepted set of assumptions. The danger of this lies in the separation of a class of people, arbitrarily assigned by psychiatry, into a position of dependence not assigned to others. Until and unless a person is convicted of a crime, he should be given equal treatment under the law—no less.

Reference

Szasz, Thomas S. (1977). *Psychiatric Slavery*. New York: The Free Press.

3

Autonomous Psychotherapy and the Ethics of Involuntary Mental Hospitalization

The practice of psychoanalysis has developed into a multitude of forms in this century. One form, as practiced and described by Dr. Thomas Szasz, is that of autonomous psychotherapy. This theory focuses on the contractual arrangement between therapist and client, wherein there is a thorough understanding by both of the process and goals sought as a result of psychotherapy. This theory falls into direct conflict with the theories of involuntary commitment of so-called mental patients. It is that conflict which will be the focus of this chapter, based on Dr. Szasz's discussion of "The Initial Contact between Patient and Therapist" (p. 153) as described in his book entitled *The Ethics of Psychoanalysis* (1974).

It is Szasz's view that only the person seeking therapy be the one allowed to make initial arrangements with the therapist. He believes that calls from relatives, friends, doctors, hospitals, or other representatives are not acceptable because they increase the chance of misunderstandings and may foster an unrealistic image of the therapist (p. 156). Although the comparison might seem unusual, obviously mental patients who are involuntarily committed are, by definition, not involved in the initial contact. This immediately creates an atmosphere of deception and coercion, both of which are totally unacceptable in autonomous psychotherapy. Szasz feels that his approach is one which puts the therapist in a position of doing something for a client, rather than to him (p. 156).

The basic elements involved in committing a person to a mental institution are the foundation for a completely non-therapeutic relationship between psychiatrist and mental patient. The person being committed has no choice in the matters of finding an appropriate therapist or establishing a working contract. His treatment, therefore, is not in any way autonomous psychotherapy (nor does it claim to be). It is Szasz's view that the client needs to be informed of the methods of the therapist, his fees, his appointment schedule, and his approach to therapy from the very beginning of the relationship (p. 157). The mental patient is relieved of these rights by institutional psychiatrists who perceive that their patients are incapable of making those decisions.

The basic requirements of an honest therapeutic environment involve the ability of a client to ask those questions which are relevant to the therapeutic relationship and be given an answer (p. 158). If a client perceives that there is a deception or an unwillingness to be frank and open on the therapist's part, then the relationship may suffer irreversible damage (p. 159). In an institutional setting, the patient is often not acknowledged to have the ability to even ask pertinent questions, and certainly is not afforded the right to be given frank and open responses to his concerns. Szasz believes strongly that autonomous psychotherapy allows the client to be in control of his situation, and that the therapist fails if he seeks to dominate the relationship (p. 163). Although it may be true that not all clients would be interested in this type of therapy, they nonetheless have a choice. Mental patients involuntarily committed have no choices and are, in a literal sense, treated similarly to convicted criminals.

The comparison between mental patients and prospective clients of psychotherapy may seem odd. However, in the context of Szasz's philosophy, it is a sound comparison for a few important reasons. The mental patient and the prospective client differ only in external definition in Szasz's frame of reference. Szasz does not believe that the mental patient is, except by definition, necessarily less capable mentally than any one else. He feels it is an arbitrary label (although a sometimes defensible one) to call someone a mental patient and one that is based socially, not therapeutically. It is quite possible for Szasz that a client seeking voluntary therapy may be more "crazy" than an involuntarily committed mental patient. Thus, the reasons ordinarily used to defend the subordination of a class of people committed to mental institutions, such as "they don't know what is best for them," or "we need to help those who can't help themselves," lose their validity in Szasz's concept. [*Ethics of Psychoanalysis,* Chapter 10]

Following the above delineated reasoning, Szasz does not believe it should ever be the role of a therapist to "participate in the patient's extra-analytic life" (p. 163). On an individual level this means not allowing the therapy to be extended beyond its contractual boundaries. The therapist does not allow himself to be used as anything other than therapist, and only during the allotted therapy time (p. 164). He should not call a patient's spouse, or doctor, for example, to satisfy some extra-analytic request. Similarly, he should never be an agent of any person other than his patient. In an institutional setting these guidelines are neither followed nor acknowledged. The mental patient is deemed to have every "right" to have his life shared with those who are attempting to "help" him. The result is that the therapist becomes an agent of many, not just the client, and the relationship between therapist and patient loses boundaries. It is difficult to imagine what an involuntarily committed patient stands to gain by being honest with a psychiatrist who is not necessarily acting in only that patient's interests.

The essential difference in approaches to treating people is in the definition and labeling attached to them at the outset of treatment. It provides a reason (excuse) for treating some patients with more or less regard than others, and is the building block upon which entire methodologies are developed. To commit a person to an institution presupposes the individual's inability to be treated in a more civilized way, and attaches a stigma to that person from which it is almost impossible to escape. Almost all individuals are capable of acting autonomously—those who are not need to be dealt with only if they have committed criminal acts.

The practice of autonomous psychotherapy is essentially antithetical to the practice of involuntary commitment. The purpose of the comparisons drawn herein is not to suggest that autonomous psychotherapy is appropriate for all patients (clients). It clearly will not serve all the possible needs of those seeking therapy. It is a clearly preferable form of treatment, though again this is not an attempt to prove that. The aim has been to describe the differences in such extreme approaches, and to provide some insight into Dr. Szasz's complete disdain for the involuntary incarceration of mental hospital patients.

Reference

Szasz, Thomas S. (1974). *The Ethics of Psychoanalysis.* New York: The Free Press.

4

The Adversarial Position of the Mentally Ill in Society

The previous chapters of this work have focused on aspects of the Szaszian philosophy which have created a great deal of controversy in psychiatric circles. The issues of defining and explaining illness, mental hospitalization and incarceration, and the role of the state in involuntary mental hospitalization are all central to an understanding of the direction of Szasz's work. In this context, the mentally ill are seen as being in an adversarial position, one in which they have been separated and classified as a group to be distinguished from the rest of the society. In this labeling process, the term "mentally ill" has become distorted, and has come to represent a wide array of people traditionally considered to be adversarial to society. This group includes such elements of society as criminals, sociopaths, and indigents.

The use of involuntary mental hospitalization as a form of imprisonment has also placed the mentally ill in an adversarial position with society. The "treatment" of the "mentally ill" in involuntary settings places incarcerated individuals in direct conflict with social authority. Any person deprived of his/her freedoms, whether described as "mentally ill" or "convicted criminal" is, of necessity, in conflict with society as long as his/her incarceration continues. In the case of involuntarily committed mental patients, the conflict is magnified by the fact that there is often disagreement over whether or not the person needs to be incarcerated. Persons adjudicated as criminals are assumed to have been given due process of law, wherein they would be convicted and jailed according to prescribed sentencing guidelines.

Rationalizations for Incarceration

There are many reasons given by doctors and the state for placing people into mental hospitals against their will. However, it is not only the psychiatrists and the state, but family members, friends, and other concerned individuals who contribute to the process. Familiar rationalizations such as "they don't realize they need help," and "they can't take care of themselves" are as much a part of the layman's vocabulary as the professional's or state's. "Common knowledge" as to what is mental illness is often relied upon by well-intentioned family or friends who describe their relative or friend as being unstable, disoriented, "crazy," or some otherwise nebulous term.

It is the responsibility of the psychiatric profession to determine whether or not individuals are, in a legal context, mentally competent. This process is greatly flawed. What are routinely described as reasons for incarcerating someone against his/her will may be better labeled rationalizations. As defined by *Webster's II New Riverside Dictionary* (1984), to rationalize is "to devise self-satisfying but incorrect explanations for (e.g., one's behavior)" (p. 580). These "self-satisfying" explanations, such as those listed in the DSM-IV, have led to the institutionalization of many citizens.

Szasz feels that many so-called psychiatric problems are problems in living and not diseases to be "cured" (1987). The rationalization that somehow involuntary mental hospitalization will produce individuals who will go on to be productive members of society is refuted by Szasz in the following remark:

> "I insist that a decent and honorable ('mentally healthy') life cannot be achieved by buying (or otherwise receiving) psychiatric treatments" (p.169).

The objective of having people become "decent and honorable" is couched in a discussion of both those terms that could go on indefinitely. The point remains, however, that to expect people's nature to change is beyond the scope of psychiatric intervention, and is not attainable through involuntary mental hospitalization.

Another rationalization used in justifying involuntary mental hospitalization is that to subject mentally ill people to criminal penalties is an oppressive act (Schoenfeld, 1976). Is placing a person in a mental hospital, where conditions are sometimes worse than in prisons, any less oppressive? While it is understandable that people who are literally incapable of comprehending criminal proceedings (due to a discernible brain dysfunction) would not be subject to criminal penalties (jail), unless such findings can be made for other mentally ill people, full rights to due process should be in place. If not, it becomes extremely difficult to establish how any person who commits crimes (especially horrible crimes) could not be insane. Such criminal acts are commonly referred to as "crazy," so it appears inconsistent to say that a person who has committed a "crazy" act is competent to stand trial under our current justice system.

Doctors as Adversaries

Doctors functioning as agents of the state are an integral aspect of the adversarial relationship between the mentally ill and society. Szasz and other civil libertarians believe that the psychiatrist forfeits his commitment to confidentiality between patient and therapist when the state (or any other third party) is involved (Szasz, 1974). In an institutional setting, the guidelines of confidentiality are neither acknowledged nor followed. The mental patient is deemed to have every "right" to have his life shared with all those who are attempting to "help" him. The result is that the therapist becomes an agent of many (e.g. the state, hospital staff, family of the patient), not just the client, and the relationship between therapist and patient loses boundaries. It is difficult to imagine what an involuntarily committed patient stands to gain by being honest with a psychiatrist who is not necessarily acting in <u>only</u> the patient's interests.

Psychiatric treatment in the context of involuntary mental hospitalization compels people to "confess by word or act of faith" (Szasz, 1977, p. 112) in order for them to escape. Once deemed to have fit a socially prescribed norm of "reality," the patient may be released. The principle of therapy being based on an honest interchange is compromised in situations involving involuntary mental hospitalization. If a person is not willing to be institutionalized and realizes that if he is honest he will be, an accurate diagnosis of him cannot be made. It would be self-incrimination for such a person to be honest in this situation (p. 123), a circumstance that would not be permitted in a court of law.

The psychiatrist may be the adversary of the involuntary mental patient when it comes to the actual administration of therapies. The results of involuntarily imposed "treatments" are not consistently effective and may sometimes be damaging. The psychiatrist's conduct "as judged by the recipients of his benevolence," exclaims Szasz, "is deemed to be not treatment, but torture, with consequences again all too familiar (1977, p.10)." This is not to say that all psychiatric interventions are necessarily ineffective in such situations, but rather to say that the likelihood of positive results is diminished by the creation of an adversarial position between psychiatrist and patient.

The Practice and Ethics of Behavior Therapy

Behavior therapy is a form of therapy that is used routinely with involuntarily committed patients who are unwilling to agree to intervention. The American Psychological Association says that permission to treat should be obtained whenever possible, but leaves the door open for treatment without permission if it is found impossible to obtain. An explanation of the methods used in behavior therapy and the questionable ethics associated with those methods is central to demonstrating the adversarial role of the mentally ill in society.

Behavior therapy (or modification) is a method by which psychiatrists and other practitioners bring the behavior of their patients under control and shape those behaviors to fit socially acceptable parameters. In prisons, for example, behavior modification is sometimes used to change behaviors in inmates so that they may gain parole—no behavior change, no parole. In such cases, refusal of an inmate to participate in a behavior modification program may be reason enough to deny parole, even though his behavior might have been good enough to be released. Similar tactics are sometimes applied to involuntary mental patients, where behavior modification can be particularly effective when considering that there is no determinate sentence after which a non-criminal mental patient must be released.

In a situation where intervention is contracted between consenting adults, an ethical relationship is established where the person seeking the contract is having his needs be the focus, not vice-versa. As the following discussion will show, behavior therapists have on numerous occasions used involuntary patients as subjects for experimentation (Szasz, 1977). Most professionals in human services would agree (one would hope) that "...it is the moral duty of psychiatrists and psychologists to safeguard the liberty and dignity of people (p.52)," and that it is criminal to use incarcerated patients as "guinea pigs." Some famous behavior therapists such as Lindsay, Skinner, and Ayllon have used their power over patients for their experiments, with sometimes damaging results.

Lindsay took non-responding (no visible reactions to therapist or staff) mental patients and used them in a behavior modification experiment, where he attempted to obtain a response by offering them cigarettes (Szasz, 1977, p.52). One patient refused to respond to the offer of a cigarette, upon which Lindsay concluded this patient to be uncooperative. The question that arises from this is how Lindsay could give up on a patient because he would not respond to a cigarette. Maybe the patient didn't like cigarettes or chose not to respond. Ayllon used starvation of patients as an experiment in changing behavior (p.54). As might be expected, the patients became easier to handle after being starved, but that obviously does not justify the tactic.

The American Psychological Association has condoned many of the questionable practices of behavior modification for some time. This includes extending involuntary hospital stays of some patients in order to help extinguish bad habits (as identified by staff members) (Szasz, 1977, p.54), using shock treatment to the genitals and nude photographs of women and children to extinguish child molesters' desires for children (p.57), and use of indeterminate sentences to "enhance cooperation" in mental patients (p.58). The indeterminate sentence was used extensively in a treatment facility called the Patuxent Institution, where its director, Dr. Arthur Kandel, is quoted to have said:

> "People respond well to the indeterminate sentence. They don't understand it's a necessary part of treatment" (p.58).

The issue of whether or not the ends justify the means is of particular significance in discussing behavior modification. The primary concern should not be the result, but whether the patient agrees to the methods.

Without governmental sponsorship, behavior therapy would not survive. In a free marketplace, competing openly with other forms of treatment, it would quickly disappear (Szasz, 1977, p. 56). Perhaps this explains why behavior therapy has taken such strong hold in involuntary mental hospitalization. It is difficult to imagine people freely agreeing to be subjected to some of the procedures described above. Without the ability to coerce involuntary subjects, and without state-sponsored grants for experiments, behavior modification would lose a great deal of its power in the psychiatric profession (p.56).

Voluntary Versus Involuntary Treatment

There is some debate among psychiatrists and other therapists over the concept of voluntary treatment and whether it actually exists. The idea that somehow all interventions are the result of some coercion, and by virtue of such coercion are not truly voluntary, is one to ponder. In Thomas Szasz's *The Theology of Medicine* (1977) he points to a study by Richard Parlout, M.D., who said that:

> "patients are coerced into treatments by pain, fear, and despair as well as by spouses, employers, and judges. Voluntary treatment is a myth" (p.59).

One difficulty with such a statement is that it classifies all treatments as involuntary but does not factor in legal aspects. A person who is legally compelled to treatment surely needs to be categorized differently, in a legal context, from a person who may come and go for treatment without coercion by the state. If not, then the issue of involuntary mental hospitalization becomes reduced to a discussion of semantics, wherein the criminal aspect is lost.

Ullman writes that therapists cannot believe in freedom of choice because there is a root to all choice—the choice came from somewhere. Szasz sees this as an excuse to intervene in a person's life (1977, p.64), and a justification for delving too deeply into someone's problems in living (p.63). Krasner writes "the therapist is always society's agent" (p.64), with which Szasz agrees and expands upon, believing this principle should be made clear to the client from the outset. Keeping interventions voluntary in a social and legal context separates them from involuntary mental hospitalization, where there is an overlap between the social, legal, and psychological aspects of the person's treatment. Such conflicting interests lead to the placement of the involuntary mental patient in an adversarial position to society that is not possible in legally voluntary interventions.

◆ ◆ ◆

The mentally ill have been assigned the role of adversary to the community at large through psychiatric, legal, social, and "scientific" attempts to classify them as a population to be treated with the understanding that they are not entitled to all the rights of the rest of society. "Professional" opinions of how to treat the mentally ill have become firmly entrenched in our laws and in our way of thinking. Until and unless actions are taken to reverse the separation of the so-called mentally ill from the rest of society in terms of legal rights, social stigma, and psychiatric incarceration, then the "mentally ill" will continue to occupy a role as society's scapegoat. The position of adversary has been imposed upon, not chosen by, the so-called mentally ill population.

References

American Psychiatric Association. (1994). *Diagnostic and Statistical Manual of Mental Disorders* (4th ed.). Washington, D.C.: Author

Schoenfeld, C.G. (1976). An Analysis of the Views of Thomas Szasz. *Journal of Psychiatry and Law. 4, 245-263.*

Szasz, Thomas. (1974). *Ceremonial Chemistry: The Ritual Persecution of Drugs, Addicts, and Pushers.* New York: Doubleday.

Szasz, Thomas. (1977). *Psychiatric Slavery.* New York: The Free Press.

Szasz, Thomas. (1977). *The Theology of Medicine.* Baton Rouge, LA: LSU Press.

Szasz, Thomas (1987), *Insanity—The Idea and Its Consequences.* New York: John Wiley and Sons.

Webster's II New Riverside Dictionary (1984). Berkley Books—Houghton—Mifflin: New York.

5

Integration of Theories and Issues

"The mad truth: the boundary between sanity and insanity is a false one. The proper outcome of psychoanalysis is the abolition of the boundary, the healing of the split, the integration of the human race. The proper posture is to listen to and learn from lunatics...The insane do not share 'the normal prejudice in favor of external reality.' The 'normal prejudice in favor of external reality' can be sustained only by ejecting (projecting) these dissidents from the human race; scotomizing them, keeping them out of sight, in asylums; insulating the so-called reality-principle from all evidence to contrary."

—Norman 0. Brown, *Love's Body*

The previous chapters of this work have been designed to present some of the major theoretical constructs that form the philosophy of Thomas Szasz. Issues such as the right to treatment, the position of the mentally ill in society, and the role of the state in involuntary mental hospitalization are all closely interconnected, and form the foundation upon which the concept of the abolition of involuntary mental hospitalization is based. It is my contention that Dr. Szasz is essentially correct in his view that all involuntary mental hospitalization of persons not convicted of a crime is a violation of basic civil liberties and rights. In a society that seeks to be truly free, such a situation should not be tolerated.

In order to appropriately integrate the theories and issues presented in this discourse, it is necessary to discuss the abolition of involuntary mental hospitalization not only from a psychological perspective, but from a social, legal, political, and criminal aspect as well. The separation of medicine and the state, the politics of involuntary mental hospitalization, and the basic civil rights of our citizens are all essential components in the formulation of a strong theory advocating the abolition of involuntary mental hospitalization. The understanding of humanism, in its truest sense, is also a vital element in the development of a theory which focuses on the validation of each human being in our society and affirms the right of the individual to be truly self-determinant (within the parameters of the law).

The abolition of involuntary mental hospitalization is a highly controversial concept. Dr. Thomas Szasz has reached his conclusions based on some fifty years of writing, researching, and participating in the psychiatric profession. His ideas, while referred to as "nutty" by the prominent psychologist Dr. Albert Ellis (Szasz & Ellis, 1977), may not be dismissed as easily by others who are truly concerned with the welfare of mental patients. An analysis of the language of mental illness, combined with observations on the nature of institutional psychiatry, has led Szasz and others to a position which, upon scrutiny, stands to reason. I believe that Szasz's position is a well-constructed, carefully analyzed and integrated one, and one which will lead to the re-establishment of the individual as a truly autonomous entity.

Abolition of Involuntary Commitment

In order to establish criteria for involuntary mental hospitalization, psychiatry, as has been shown, needed to develop a system of practices which appeared to be scientific in nature. The accomplishment of this goal has elevated psychiatry to a position where its findings and opinions are treated as scientific facts. The status enjoyed by the psychiatric profession has allowed it to maintain a system of involuntary mental hospitalization that is difficult to imagine existing in a country such as the United States. Nonetheless, such is the case, and with the support of the criminal justice and legal professions, involuntary mental hospitalization is still a viable and thriving enterprise.

Many defenders of involuntary mental hospitalization claim that "mental health is more important than personal freedom" (Szasz, 1977, p.134), and that psychiatric interventions are necessary for the protection of the individual and the society. The problem with this, however, is in determining whether or not society is being threatened by a certain individual, and in what way. Legally speaking, the mental patient is "an innocent person incarcerated in a psychiatric prison" (p. 136) and, as such, should not be subject to criminal-type sanctions. The only position with moral foundation on the issue of involuntary mental hospitalization, in the context of our societal structure, is for the complete abolition of any citizen's <u>compulsion</u> to be in a mental hospital (p.137).

In our system of justice, the individual has an inalienable right to pursue personal liberty unless he has been convicted of a criminal offense in a court of law. In the Szaszian context, involuntary mental hospitalization places great restraint on individual expression and self-determination, without just legal cause (1977, p.139). What Szasz has termed the "therapeutic rape of the patient by the psychiatrist" (1987, p.169), namely coerced interventions, are a threat to the personal freedoms of all citizens. Involuntary interventions "are not cures but coercions" (p.169) and should be rejected by psychiatrists. Coercions, when performed by representatives of the state, are a political act, and should be viewed as such. To not do so is to miss the essential nature of coercion in involuntary mental hospitalization and possible extension into other areas of social and political control.

Another fallacy sometimes presented as support for the involuntary institutionalization of mental patients is the idea that if "patients" can be treated and improved or cured, then hospitalization against their will is a good idea. I believe this is a case of the ends justifying the means—the aims of treatments or interventions cannot be justified based on their perceived curative ability. Additionally, the patient is placed into a very self-incriminating position when confronted by institutional psychiatrists. As previously stated, if a person is unwilling to be institutionalized and realizes that if he is honest he will be, an accurate diagnosis of him cannot be given.

To remove the compulsion to be in a mental hospital is analogous, in some ways, to the repeal of slavery. In removing the compulsion to be there, the mental patient may choose to leave, but he also may choose to <u>stay.</u> Voluntary treatments, when consented to by adults, are part of a citizen's rights. In much the same way, the repeal of slavery did not force slaves to leave their homes if they chose not to. It is the process of emancipation that is essential in the regaining of individual rights, and a process which would be destroyed by placing new or additional restrictions on that freedom. To claim to know what is best for a person is to support the contentions of many institutional psychiatrists and social theorists that it is ultimately in the best interest of society for such judgments to be made. I dispute that contention, and agree with Szasz's view that equal treatment under the law for all citizens is fundamental to a free and just society (1977).

Validating Involuntary Mental Hospitalization by Advocating Change

By arguing for the improvement or alteration of a system, whatever it may be, there is an implied notion that by advocating change the system should continue to exist. In order to end involuntary mental hospitalization, the system of incarcerating mental patients does not require change, it requires termination. Advocating changes in the system legitimizes its existence (Szasz, 1977). On a purely practical level, any changes that would help the involuntary patient on a short-term basis are welcome, but on an ideological level, advocating change in the system distorts and dampens the argument against involuntary mental hospitalization. Since the desired result is no less than complete abolition, then ideologically no effort should be spent on reform (p. 90).

The goal in eliminating involuntary mental hospitalization is to restore the concept that all citizens not convicted of crimes should be treated equally under the law. The advocacy of changes such as replacing psychiatric hospitals with other forms of "psychiatric repression" (Szasz, 1977, p.90), for example clinics for involuntary patients, accomplishes nothing constructive. While intending to improve the lot of the involuntary mental patient, legal writers have somewhat damaged the cause of abolishing involuntary mental hospitalization by seeming to make it more palatable. Unfortunately, no matter how it is "dressed up," involuntary mental hospitalization remains a violation of basic civil liberties, which many legal scholars will acknowledge in only a roundabout way. The following statement serves to articulate the type of legal rhetoric that attempts to make involuntary mental hospitalization seem both reasonable and practical:

> "It is suggested that the most progressive, humane, and realistic attitude on the part of the state would be to abolish both capital punishment and the insanity defense and provide a statutory right to adequate treatment for everyone confined in state institutions, whether civil or penal" (Marschall, 1973, p.61).

While I would agree wholeheartedly with the abolition of capital punishment and the insanity defense, I find an inconsistency in Marschall's thinking on right to treatment issues. It is difficult to understand why Marschall advocates the continued existence of civil institutions if all accused criminals would no longer have the option of being put in a civil institution, by virtue of removing the insanity defense. Civil institutions might then be used to control "social deviants" who have not been convicted of any crimes.

Separation of Medicine and the State

The state's involvement in medicine, particularly in psychiatry, takes the primary responsibility for the individual's health from him and places it with the government. The state entrusts the psychiatrist with the power to make decisions about a person's competence and his potential incarceration. The psychiatrist is asked to use his "best judgment" (Katz, 1969, p.782) regarding a patient's health, and is not expected to gain "informed consent" (p.782) from a person deemed to be mentally unstable. The risks of relative consequences of treatments do not need to be discussed with an involuntary mental patient in state-imposed "therapies." The goal of separating medicine and the state can only be accomplished by recognizing and honoring the rights of the individual.

The state's authority in matters of involuntary mental hospitalization has been supported by what was in 1921 referred to as the Association of Medical Superintendents of American Institutions for the Insane, now known as the American Psychiatric Association, whose first official proposition was:

> "Resolved, that it is the unanimous sense of this convention that the attempt to abandon entirely the use of all means of personal restraint is not sanctioned by the true interests of the insane" (Szasz, 1973, p.135).

The continued professional support of state-sponsored involuntary mental hospitalization provides the essential elements necessary for survival. Those elements include fostering the sense among the citizens that this practice is founded on solid scientific principles, and that involuntary mental hospitalization is a benevolent act supported by professionals who, after all, are supposed to be in the business of helping people. Public opinion toward involuntary mental hospitalization would almost certainly change if psychiatry refused to sanction this practice any longer.

If there were no mental health laws which create a separate "category of individuals who, though officially labeled as mentally ill, would prefer not to be subjected to involuntary psychiatric interventions" (Szasz, p.137), then the abuses that occur in caring for mental patients could not occur without recourse. This is true for the reason that mental patients would be subject to protection by laws that apply to <u>all</u> citizens, including protection of fundamental civil rights. The individuals responsible for creating and enforcing laws regarding involuntary mental hospitalization, should, in this context, be regarded as the "adversaries, not allies, of the mental patient" (p. 137).

The issue of separating medicine and the state would not be adequately discussed without pointing out the role of the citizenry in the continuation of involuntary mental hospitalization. The treatments and practices legally carried out by psychiatrists working in state-sponsored institutions are supported by society and, hence, by those individuals who form the society. Any harm that is done to people as a result of involuntary mental hospitalization is the responsibility, in part, of society, because the society (as represented by the state) endorses involuntary mental hospitalization and pays professionals to work with involuntary patients. I believe that the practice of involuntary mental hospitalization could not survive a massive public outcry, and would not continue to exist if pressure were brought to bear on society's representatives.

True Humanism

> "If we value personal freedom and dignity, we should, in confronting the moral dilemmas of biology, genetics, and medicine, insist that the expert's allegiance to the agents and values he serves be made explicit and that the power inherent in his specialized knowledge and skill not be accepted as justification for his exercising specific controls over those lacking such knowledge and skill."
>
> —Thomas Szasz, *The Theology of Medicine*

In Chapter One, I presented a brief overview of humanism in the Szaszian context. In integrating the theories and issues presented subsequently, the concept of humanism in its true form has been developed and expanded upon. Humanistic principles, such as personal autonomy and the right to dissent, are the ideological foundation of Szasz's work, from which his insistence on the abolition of involuntary mental hospitalization is based. Central to this construct are the rights of the individual, including the right to self-determination and the right to be treated equally under the law.

Szasz is concerned with humanism as an ideal that our society should strive to grasp and implement. He sees definitions of humanism such as Webster's "devotion to human welfare: interest in concern for man," and "a doctrine, set of attitudes, or way of life centered upon human interests and values" (1976, p. 1100), as being so framed as to "command universal assent" (Szasz, 1977, p.86). Szasz believes that these definitions are of little benefit, since they do not allow for both agreement and dissent to "humanistic" principles (p.87). The term "humanism" in the context of these definitions is a tautology and, as such, does not allow for reasonable debate over what humanism truly is.

Language and Humanism

In order to qualify as a humanist in Szasz's model, the proper use of language is essential (1977, p.88). It is paramount in order to convey ideas in a clear and precise manner. While the proper use of language will not automatically qualify an individual as a humanist in Szasz's framework, it is a necessary component of humanistic tradition.

Language is very important when applied to the field of psychiatry, and its abuse has been a source of continued irritation to those who practice its careful utilization. For example, the generally accepted definition of schizophrenia is "a mental disease whose principle manifestation or symptom is a disturbance in thinking" (Szasz, p.89, italic added). How, then is "thinking" defined? Kolb's Noyes' *Modern Clinical Psychiatry* (1968), defines thinking as follows:

> "The joining of ideas one to another by imagining, conceiving, inferring, and other processes, and the formation of new ideas by these processes, constitute the function we know as thinking" (p.95).

Sometimes mental patients do talk in an unconventional way, but that does not necessarily mean that their thinking is disordered. Freud and Jung both believed that mental patients do not talk gibberish, "but rather may speak in a metaphorical manner which we do not understand" (p.89). I believe that in addition to our ability to understand, if we do not like what a person is saying, we also tend to qualify such speech as mental illness.

The term "schizophrenia" was popularized by Bleuler in 1911 in his famous monograph entitled "Dementia Praecox, or the Group of Schizophrenias." He described schizophrenia as a disease which "is characterized by a specific type of alteration in thinking" (p.9). For Szasz, this terminology is an abuse of language designed to give scientific legitimacy to the characterization that "lunatics are irrational" (Szasz, p.90). Blueler went on to say that the content of the language qualifies a person as schizophrenic (p.147), to which Szasz reacts with his contention that the language of many so-called schizophrenics is "laden with metaphors that are unacceptable to those listening, especially psychiatrists" (p.91).

The psychiatric community claims a desire to better understand their patients, but is it simply a matter of understanding or also of control? An interesting claim made by some psychiatrists is that while a person's behavior may seem incomprehensible, it is more easily understood by psychiatrists than by that person himself (Szasz, p.95). This apparent contradiction is the basis upon which many diagnoses are offered and interventions undertaken. While many psychiatrists who participate in this process call themselves humanists, they do not act as such. The affirmation of the human being as uniquely individual and the rejection of control over our fellow citizens are essentially humanistic viewpoints. The adherence to a doctrine of control by language should be viewed with skepticism, and should be challenged whenever possible.

The purpose of a discussion of language and humanism is to demonstrate that it is not enough for us to rely on our intuitive judgments of people based on the way they express themselves. In compelling people to explain and describe themselves in a manner found satisfactory to psychiatrists, we place those people in a position of being judged based on the way they use language. Szasz has written:

> "They (psychiatrists)—insist that the patient give them an account of himself satisfactory to them—and if the patient fails to do so, they declare him to be ill and imprison him as insane" (1977, p.94).

Szasz believes that it is essential for "all humanists to realize the dual function of language" (p.95), which is for purposes of not only understanding people, but for controlling them. It is the true humanist position to be aware of and refuse to participate in the abuse of language.

Self-determination and the Right to Dissent

In discussing issues such as the rights of the mentally ill, a very important point is frequently overlooked. In advocating the rights of a particular group of people, the individuality of those people is obscured by the label attached to them. In the context of true humanism, it is the right of the individual to reject any labels that he so chooses (excepting that of a convicted criminal). As Thomas Szasz has stated:

> "We should stand steadfast for the right of men and women to reject those involuntary identifications or diagnoses that have traditionally justified and made possible, and often continue to justify and make possible, their inferior or subhuman treatment at the

hands of those who ostensibly care for them but who actually scapegoat them" (1977, p.96).

It is a direct contradiction to call oneself a humanist and continue to "preach and practice" (Szasz, p.96) any form of discrimination. Fundamental to the humanist approach is that each individual has the right to be treated as a self-determinant human being, provided he or she is an adult and is acting within the boundaries of the law. This means that individuals have the right to refuse treatment if they so desire and that all people, regardless of how different they might be from us, have the right to be treated as "a priori [no] better or worse" (p.96). These rights come with corresponding obligations, and remain intact as long as the person lives up to those responsibilities. To put it another way, not only do "victims" of involuntary mental hospitalization have the right to be treated with dignity, they have the obligation to <u>expect</u> to be treated as equal to other citizens and to be responsible for their own participation in society.

Each member of society who has no current criminal convictions against him has the right, so we are told, to self-determination. If this were genuinely true, how then could we justify involuntary mental hospitalization? We could not, but yet involuntary mental hospitalization does exist. Some limitations on the right to self-determination go beyond criminal considerations. The use of rhetoric to justify incarceration is rampant. The protection of people from themselves, the removal of "potentially dangerous" citizens, the protection of people who are too sick to realize that they are ill, etc.—all these excuses and rationalizations are presented for our approval, which we as a society accept with open arms, perhaps not realizing the potential for disaster in such a stance.

As indicated in Chapter One, the Szaszian concept of humanism includes a right of the individual to speak out in dissent. In the former Soviet Union, dissenters had been categorized as "mentally ill" and confined to institutions (Szasz, p.147). Is it not possible that under our current system of state-sponsored involuntary mental hospitalization such abuses could occur (or are occurring)? To place the dissenter in a position of adversary to society is to place him in a similar position to the involuntary mental patient.

The ability of the state to potentially eliminate dissent by finding dissidents "mentally ill" is convenient in many ways. The rights of due process are not as crucial a consideration in attempting to control dissent through involuntary mental hospitalization as they would be in a criminal context. The placement of dissenting individuals in a mental hospital is quite palatable if perceived by society as removal of a "crazy" person. It is a politically expedient tool, and one which could be used (or might currently be used) to control some forms of dissent. It seems that the overriding concern is that while the use of involuntary mental hospitalization to control dissent may not as yet be a widespread practice, the potential for increased abuse is there. This is unacceptable in the humanist concept, and should be more seriously considered by society at large.

Institutional psychiatry is an inherently political hazard. As such, the rhetoric of politics and the language of coercion are essential elements of the process. George Orwell has said of political language that it "is designed to make lies sound truthful and murder respectable, and to give an appearance of solidity to pure wind" In the Szaszian concept of humanism, psychiatry occupies the realm of politics and fits Orwell's description very well. Psychiatry, in the political sense, is the enemy of humanism. Its doctrines of mental disorders and the coercive nature of involuntary mental hospitalization make psychiatry a powerful foe of humanism. Psychiatry has provided a way to describe unusual behavior in terms of illness, and has succeeded in distorting the famous phrase "I am a man, nothing human is alien to me" into "I am a psychiatrist, nothing alien is human to me" (Szasz, p.98).

The integration of theories and issues on the abolition of involuntary mental hospitalization is a complex process. The positions taken herein should not be mistaken to mean that there are no individuals in need of help or that assistance should not be available to those who choose it. Rather, it is to say that involuntary mental hospitalization, as it exists currently, has no place in a free society such as we like to believe ours strives to be. It is a system which separates and removes the rights of a group of citizens who are guilty of no crime. It is based on psychiatric principles which I, and many others, believe are not well founded and are certainly fallible. In light of such obvious contradictions with the rest of our societal beliefs, it is clear that involuntary mental hospitalization should be abolished.

The following statement from Thomas Szasz's *The Theology of Medicine* (1977), while containing a harsh condemnation of psychiatry that may go beyond many of his followers' opinions, nonetheless provides some questions and comments that are worthy of serious consideration:

> "We saw it happen in Nazi Germany, and we hanged many of the doctors. We see it happen in the Soviet Union, and we denounce the doctors with righteous indignation. But when will we see that the same things are happening in the so-called free societies? When will we recognize—and publicly identify—the medical criminals among us? Or is the very possibility of perceiving many of our leading psychiatrists and psychiatric institutions in that way precluded by the fact that they represent the officially correct views and practices; by the fact that they have the ears of our lawyers and legislators, journalists and judges; and by the fact that they control the vast funds, collected by the state through taxing citizens, that finance an enterprise whose basic moral legitimacy I have called into question? (p.139).

The questioning of our institutions, be they civil, political, or psychiatric, is of great significance to the maintenance of social justice, and is the originating point of social reform. Our willingness to be diligent in the pursuit of social justice will determine whether or not such equity will prevail.

References

Katz, Jay. (1969). *The Right to Treatment—An Enchanting Legal Fiction?* University of Chicago Law Review. 36. 755-263.

KoIb, L.C. (1968). *Noyes Modern Clinical Psychiatry,* 7th Ed. Saunders: Philadelphia.

Marschall, Patricia H. (1973). A Critique of the "Right To Treatment" Approach. In a Grant H. Morris (Ed.) *The Mentally Ill and the Right To Treatment* (37-62). Springfield, IL: Thomas.

Medicine and the State: The First Amendment Violated. An Interview with Thomas Szasz. (1973) *TheHumanist. 33,* 4-9.

Szasz, Thomas. (1977). *Psychiatric Slavery.* New York: The Free Press.

Szasz, Thomas. (1977). *The Theology of Medicine.* Baton Rouge, LA: LSU Press.

Szasz, Thomas (1987). *Insanity—The idea and Its Consequences.* New York: John Wiley and Sons.

Szasz, Thomas S. & Ellis, Albert (Speakers). (1977). *Mental Illness: Fact or Myth* (Cassette Tape). Baldwin, N.Y.: W.E. Simon.

Webster's II New Riverside Dictionary (1984). Berkley Books—Houghton—Mifflin: New York

6

Responsibility of the Community at Large

Ultimately, the responsibility for controlling the way society treats its citizens rests with the community at large. This community includes people from all walks of life, including both professionals and lay people, all of whom have something at stake in deciding the direction our society is to take. It is often easier to blame others for our predicaments, but if we can transcend that rationalization we are left with the reality that it is the responsibility of the community as a whole to control abuses and to stop destructive actions. When it comes to involuntary mental hospitalization, the responsibility of the entire society is clear.

Thomas Szasz believes that "all of our traditional efforts to bring about 'psychiatric reforms' have been misconceived and misdirected" (1987, p.171). In discussing what should be done to improve psychiatric imprisonment, we confuse two different "problems and questions" (p.171), as articulated by Szasz:

1. "What are the proper or improper uses of psychiatry?" and
2. "Should psychiatric practice be based on the principle of paternalism (legitimizing virtually unlimited psychiatric power) or on the principle of contract (rendering such power illegitimate)?" (p.171).

The community at large must decide whether or not it is simply enough to be satisfied with actions designed to curb psychiatric "abuses." If that is enough (as it currently seems to be), then permission is being granted to the psychiatric profession to continue its paternalistic practices, so long as they do so within certain limits. How do we truly know what psychiatric "abuse" is, and is it possible to decide in a nonpolitical or "morally unbiased way" (Szasz, p.172) what constitutes psychiatric abuse? It is essential for the community at large to consider these questions and to realize that the power to answer them should not rest exclusively with the psychiatric profession. It is an historically proven principle that those in power (in this case, psychiatrists) tend to view their use of power as good, while the subjugated perceive the wielding of that same power as bad (p.172).

The only way to control the practices of the psychiatric profession (or any group in power) is by limiting its power. A reduction of power is tantamount to successful reform. In the case of psychiatry and involuntary mental hospitalization, curtailing the power to incarcerate people against their will places the practice of involuntary mental hospitalization squarely back into the political realm, where discussion and open debate on the practice may lead to desperately needed reforms. Psychiatry has been placed, whether by its own design or not, into a position of exclusive power over involuntary commitments. Lord Acton's insights into power, namely that power corrupts and absolute power corrupts even more (Szasz, p. 172), tell us that in our less than perfect world, power requires limits. In this sense, society takes the burden of responsibility from whomever it grants excessive power.

As part of a large community, psychiatrists and others in the behavioral sciences have a responsibility to assess the impact of their work on the society and to question and act upon their positions on relevant issues. This should include further scrutiny of the concepts of mental health and mental illness, and the impact that implementation of these constructs has on the community as a whole. If these terms are to be used as tools for separating the so-called mentally ill from the rest of society, then they are seriously lacking. The use of the terminology of mental illness to justify involuntary mental hospitalization needs to be carefully examined by psychiatrists and ordinary citizens alike, and should not be used as rationalization for some of the previously discussed violent acts committed in the name of "therapy."

Involuntary Hospitalization as Economic Boon

It is difficult to disregard the fact that involuntary mental hospitalization is an economic success for psychiatry. Many psychologists and psychiatrists currently funded by the community (through tax dollars) would be less well off than they currently are if funding were discontinued. While I am not trying to suggest that the practice of involuntary mental hospitalization is a scheme designed by psychiatrists to "pad" their wallets, I do believe that the economics of state-sponsored psychiatry is a very real issue. The almost unquestioningly accepted opinion by the community and insurance companies to grant psychiatry status as a genuine medical discipline has led to tremendous economic incentive.

Most of the money spent on community mental health is taken from the tax base (Szasz, 1988, p. 30). As such, it should be the responsibility of the community and its representatives to determine how public mental health should function, if at all. Thomas Szasz believes that psychiatrists benefit from the images of psychiatric illness and treatment used to justify the spending of public moneys (p.30). While I do concur with Szasz's opinion, I do not believe that psychiatrists are necessarily intent on gaining wealth at the expense of their patients, but are instead attempting to protect their economic future by advocating reform rather than abolition of practices such as involuntary mental hospitalization. It seems obvious that psychiatrists have a stake in proving that their profession is worthy of high regard (and corresponding economic reward). As indicated by Irwin Savodnick's statement in his review of Szasz's *Ceremonial Chemistry* (1985):

> "It is hard to ignore the fact that it is very much in the interest of psychiatry to have drug abuse and alcoholism identified as mental illnesses, just as it is very much in the interest of clergymen and policemen to have sinners and lawbreakers" (p.16).

Challenging Psychiatry and Involuntary Mental Hospitalization

The work of Thomas Szasz has been predicated on the idea that psychiatry is an inexact discipline and should be treated as such. It is with a willingness to challenge psychiatric principles and practices that abuses may be discovered and stopped. In the case of involuntary mental hospitalization, the suspension of fundamental rights of mental patients is an abuse that needs to be ended. The arguments for the abolition of laws compelling the individual to be in a mental hospital are many, but are largely based on the fundamental principles of individual liberty and the right to self-determination.

I have argued throughout this work for the abolition of all involuntary commitment to mental institutions. I believe that there are fundamental flaws in the current involuntary mental hospitalization structure, including:

1. conflicts of interest between the state, psychiatrists, and so-called psychiatric patients;

2. a removal of basic rights and civil liberties from an arbitrarily defined group of people;

3. a concentration of power in the hands of the psychiatric profession; and

4. the failure to actually provide any proven reliable methods of identifying and treating mental hospital patients.

I believe that Szasz is correct in his contention that the current system is so fundamentally flawed it is not worthy of adjustment, but should instead be abolished.

The current involuntary mental hospitalization system places a great deal of reliance on a field within which there is a tremendous divergence of opinion. There is an inherent danger in this—that of elevating the field of psychiatry to a status in which its foundations may not be questioned. By allowing psychiatry to occupy a position of such immense power, we legitimize its status and accept its attempt to define itself into an unquestioned, wholly accepted set of assumptions. A further concern lies in the separation of a class of people, arbitrarily assigned by psychiatry, into a position of dependence not assigned to others. Until and unless a person is convicted of a crime, he/she should be given equal treatment under the law—no less.

Psychiatry as a voluntary relationship between consenting adults is a perfectly acceptable practice in our society, in both legal and ethical terms. The call for the abolition of involuntary mental hospitalization is not intended to be construed as a call for the elimination of all psychiatric interventions. It is intended, however, to challenge the psychiatric community to examine its position on the issue, and to raise serious doubts about the legitimacy of psychiatry as a science. If people choose to <u>want</u> to participate in psychiatric activities, then it would be hypocritical to advocate preventing them, and would be no more acceptable in the context of individual rights than forcing them into involuntary mental hospitalization.

"Human culture never stops being religious, no matter how 'secular' it becomes" (Roszak, 1978, p.51). These words ring particularly true in the case of psychiatry and involuntary mental hospitalization, where the doctors have replaced the clerics as moral oppressors and state-sponsored social redeemers. Many psychiatrists and helping professionals, realizing how much psychiatry has grown in power and status, have begun to question the almost omnipotent nature of psychiatric dogma, and have become increasingly uncomfortable with it (Coleman, unpublished). Many professionals are now questioning the abuse of power by psychiatry (Coleman, p.55), with parts of the community at large standing directly behind them. By challenging psychiatry and not permitting a type of "blind-faith" approach toward its principles, society can contribute to the balancing of power between psychiatry and the people.

The following quote is a call for society to confront psychiatric principles that I believe addresses the fundamental elements of such a challenge:

> "What is needed is a wider recognition by the general public of how easily psychiatric opinion becomes a strategy more than a finding, as well as an appreciation of how easily psychiatric opinion becomes 'prescriptive' rather than 'descriptive'" (Coleman, p. 54).

To call for the abolition of involuntary mental hospitalization is an essential element in the challenge of psychiatric "prescriptions." It is based on the concern for preserving the rights of the individual, and protecting the rights of all members of society to be free from social or moral dogma. In recognizing and accepting that psychiatry is imposing its perception of reality on the rest of society, we see the difficulty in allowing it so much power. The challenge lies in the realization that we all are biased toward our own values, with psychiatry being no exception.

Through its attempts to be recognized as a science, psychiatry has abandoned the principals of individual differences and personal liberties. The apparent conflicts that arise in trying to categorize individuals in neatly defined scientific packages are defined out of existence in psychiatric "science." Once doubt is removed from the process of diagnosing patients, there can be little questioning of a doctor's findings. By defining doubt away, it becomes extremely difficult to challenge psychiatry, unless the principles underlying the "science" are challenged. My attempt has been to demonstrate that such challenges are warranted, even demanded by the continued abuse of the involuntary mental patient, and should be fervently undertaken by all concerned members of society.

The abolition of involuntary mental hospitalization requires the combined efforts of both the professional and lay communities. The responsibilities of the community at large to accept the challenge, and of the professional community to deal directly with such a challenge, is an immediate one. It is no longer acceptable for society to abdicate the responsibility of preserving personal liberties. Reform will only come about as a result of social pressure on both psychiatry and government. Until such time as involuntary mental incarceration is stopped, we all run the risk of becoming its victim, either by becoming directly involved in the system, or by allowing the continued erosion of our most basic civil liberties.

References

Coleman, Lee (1985); Using Psychiatry to Fight 'Cults': Three Case Histories." In a Broch K. Kilborne (Ed.), *Scientific Research and New Religions: Divergent Perspectives; vol. 2, Part 2* (p.40-56). San Francisco, CA: Pacific division, American Association for the Advancement of Science.

Roszak, Theodore. (1978) Ethics, Ecstasy, and the Study of New Religions. In a G. Baker & J. Needleman (Eds.), *Understanding the New Religions* (pp. 49-62). New York: Seabury Press.

Savodnik, Irwin. (1985). (Review of *Ceremonial Chemistry*). *The Psychiatric Times,* June 1985, 16-17.

Szasz, Thomas (1987). *Insanity—The Idea and Its Consequences.* New York: John Wiley and Sons.

Szasz, Thomas. (1988). Homelessness is Not a Disease. *USA Today.* March, pp 28-29.

7

"Medicine and the State: A Humanist Interview"

The following discussion will recount a recorded conversation between the noted psychiatrists Dr. Paul Kurtz and Dr. Thomas Szasz, a transcript of which appears in Szasz's book *The Theology of Medicine* (1977). As the title suggests, the two men explore the intermingling of the medical and legal professions, and the role of the state in regulating medical practices in the United States. As is also suggested, the subject is approached from a "humanist" perspective, as defined by Dr. Szasz as a philosophy of increasing the autonomy of the individual and allowing for free dissent in a truly free society (p. 145). It is with this philosophy in mind that the discussion proceeded, and led to some highly controversial solutions to modern social problems.

Dr. Szasz, when asked what the key value is that he tried to defend in his work, responded by saying "individual self-determination of freedom, in a political sense" (p. 145). He continued in saying that freedom is only an issue when its loss is threatened by entities that fall under the categories of the bureaucratic, paternalistic, or therapeutic state (p. 145). Szasz feels that the connection between medicine and the state is inherently dangerous, especially when it comes to the widespread acceptance of psychiatry as a "genuine medical discipline" (p. 145). It is dangerous because it mistakes the social control of autonomous behaviors for treatment of so-called medical illness, and uses "therapy" to regulate morality. According to Szasz, "medicine now functions as a state religion much as, for example, Roman Catholicism did in medieval Spain" (p. 146).

The questions posed by Dr. Kurtz throughout this conversation allowed Szasz the freedom to pursue his thesis quite cogently. When Kurtz asked, for example, why Szasz felt that there is "an unholy alliance" between medicine and the state, Szasz responded by elaborating on his opinions regarding the regulation of the medical profession by the state. The state determines what is and is not an acceptable form of medical treatment, and it is the state that must bear the responsibility for sanctioning involuntary mental hospitalization as a so-called form of medical intervention. If state law did not allow mental hospitalization on an involuntary basis, it could not exist.

> "I have been interested in involuntary mental hospitalization not only because it is such a blatant violation of human rights, but also because it reveals so clearly how we have medicalized certain moral and political problems. If someone wants to do something we really don't like—such as killing himself—then we say he is depressed and lock him up in a mental hospital. How is that possible? Because psychiatry says that depression is a disease; obviously, if you are an American, you should want to live. Look how similar that is to people's being locked up in a mental hospital in the Soviet Union because they criticize the system. Obviously, to the Soviet state and its psychiatrists, anyone who publicly expressed political dissent must be crazy; if he weren't crazy, he would be an obedient communist" (p. 147).

All involuntary mental hospitalization is inherently political, because it is used as a power over the citizen by the state, aimed at stopping dissenting behavior. In this sense, the therapeutic state is alive and well (or sick, as the case might be).

One of Dr. Szasz's more controversial views is addressed in this discussion, namely that the licensing of the medical profession be taken from the state. Szasz states "I do not believe…that the state should support…any kind of medical education" (p. 150). By supporting only certain forms of medical treatment, other possible solutions to medical problems are discarded or discredited. The freedom to choose treatments in a non-government regulated industry would create a free economic marketplace that would eventually rid itself of fraud through economic failure. In this system, the universities would set the standards in medicine, just as they do in mathematics or engineering. The point is to completely separate medicine from the state in order to allow for maximum personal freedom.

The idea of no licensing of doctors might initially seem "crazy" to many people. Szasz believes in this idea based on his contention that "the idea that licensing doctors protects the public is one of the most uncritically accepted falsehoods of our day" (p. 151). The suggestion is that the licensing of doctors is primarily for the protection of the professionals themselves, not the patients. It is a method of controlling competition, whereby numbers of physicians can be carefully regulated. To suggest that the public needs protection from quacks and frauds is valid, but does not the public also need protection from "bad parents and children, husbands and wives, mothers-in-law, bureaucrats, teachers, politicians—the list is endless" (p. 152).

We are all exposed to many factors in our lives that are potentially harmful but cannot all be regulated. The people must be able to protect themselves. Any truly free society exposes itself to risks and corresponding responsibilities. Consumers and other public-interest groups could unite to establish a system of non-governmental oversight. The problem nowadays is that very few people are even interested in thinking along those lines.

In accordance with his views on licensing of doctors, Dr. Szasz also feels that there should be no controlled substances in medicine—that is, no prescriptions. "I don't see," says Szasz, "how anyone can take seriously the idea of personal self-determination and responsibility and not insist on his right to take anything he wants to take" (p. 154). We are exposed to many dangerous substances in our everyday lives that we are entrusted with, such as lye, paint thinners, gasoline, etc., so why are drugs restricted for adult consumption? The government has no right to enforce this, yet it is allowed and accepted by the overwhelming majority of citizens. In a truly free society, a person has the right to destroy (or heal) himself with drugs if he so chooses:

> "...I would let the individual suffer the consequences rather than punish the whole society by prohibiting the 'abused' substance" (p. 155).

People cannot and should not be protected from themselves. The breakdown of morals and "family values" in our society should not be used to excuse the idea of treating our entire population as children. The ultimate responsibility for a person's well-being rests *with that person*, no one else.

Szasz is completely opposed to the accumulation of power of any one social body to the exclusion of others. He believes that power is especially dangerous when garnered under the auspices of benevolence. "Power for doing good—for good reasons—is most dangerous of all" (p. 158), and is so because it presumes that all attempts to subvert that power are not good. People should be able to express dissent to power figures or structures without being morally evaluated. This is why power is best distributed freely and is not concentrated among so-called "protectors" of the people, such as doctors and state regulating bodies.

To summarize the views of Dr. Thomas Szasz on medicine and the state, it is essential to include the concept of humanism which Szasz has developed. Humanism has distinct political elements, one of the most critical being the right to dissent:

> "...I think we should think of it (humanism) more as the right to disagree with and reject authority—religious authority, educational authority, medical authority—and of course the right to take one's chances with one's own judgment and decision" (p.162).

This definition is an affirmation of the individual and of the rights of the citizen in a free society. For Szasz, there is nothing more essential to the development of human beings.

Reference

Szasz, Thomas. (1977) *The Theology of Medicine.* Baton Rouge, La.: LSU Press.

8

Mental Illness—A Debate Between Dr. Albert Ellis and Dr. Thomas Szasz

The opportunity to hear a debate between two prominent theorists in the field of psychiatry with opinions and philosophies as divergent as those of Dr. Thomas Szasz and Dr. Albert Ellis is rare. This event, however, has been made available through an audio tape simply entitled Mental Illness, which was recorded in 1977 in Baldwin, New York. It was a fiery debate between the two theorists, and brings clearly into focus the differences between the two men. Of these differences, some of the most crucial are surrounding the issue of involuntary mental hospitalization and on the use of labels that allow for the classification of the mentally ill.

In his opening, Dr. Szasz remarks that he uses language very carefully and considers himself to be an expert in the field of operational linguistics. He also explains that he believes words are best defined by their social consequences; that is, as social consequences of a word change, then its meaning is changed. This is, in effect, an operational definition. Szasz uses the example of the word "Jew." He says that the word has totally different meanings in modern-day Israel as opposed to Nazi Germany during the reign of the Third Reich. The word is the same, but its meaning is determined by the social atmosphere of the time.

To Szasz, the term "mental illness" is a metaphor, another important distinction from literal meaning. Literal illness is what medical doctors diagnose and treat; physical or anatomical disturbances. Literal illnesses can exist even if a person is dead—i.e. a corpse can still have cancer, but can a corpse still have agoraphobia? Szasz goes on to say that not all people who are sick are patients and vice-versa. This is important in the context of mental illness because psychiatry assumes that all patients being treated are necessarily, to some degree, sick. Many patients are not sick, and many sick people are not patients. It is a "social role" to be a patient, says Szasz, and has no logical connection with the presence of disease.

There are four permutations of the patient and disease model, as follows:

1. Patient has a disease
2. No patient, no disease (healthy)
3. Not a patient, but have a disease
4. Patient, but has no disease (basis of psychology)

Szasz believes that psychiatrists are not doctors and should not use medical terms to describe their work. He says "hysterics fake illness, psychiatrists fake doctoring." Mental illness may exist in Szasz's framework, but not as a disease based on a medical model. He believes that applying the word "sick" to mental patients is to use a metaphor—one which is taken literally by psychology. We are prone to use the word "sick" to describe malfunctioning television sets or automobile engines, but we do not call doctors to repair them. We realize we are using a metaphor.

Psychology, by believing in metaphor as truth, misses the dichotomy between disease and deviance. Psychology presumes what the purpose of life is, and seeks to impose that purpose on those who are not in agreement, much like many religions. Szasz calls psychology "religion as science" and says that "it is not reasonable to say what the purpose of life is." He believes that therapy is, therefore, not a medical treatment, but is a form of intervention that is valid only on an individual basis. If the medical model is not valid when applied to psychology, then therapies and treatments can only be gauged effective on a purely existential level.

Ellis vs. Szasz—Questions and Answers

Throughout this debate, Dr. Ellis resorted to tactics that were based on the idea of discrediting Dr. Szasz personally, rather than producing solid counter-arguments to Szasz's views. Several times he referred to Szasz as "nutty" (not quite a scientific term), and continually used profanity to accentuate his points. These strategies were very ineffective and took a great deal away from the substantive aspects of Dr. Ellis' responses. However, even with these distractions, the question and answer period proved quite provocative.

In 1977, the famous case of David Berkowitz, better known as "Son of Sam," was in the headlines. A couple of questions came up regarding this case, with Ellis taking the position that Berkowitz should be placed in a mental institution where his chances of release would be much lower than if he were imprisoned. Ellis felt that Berkowitz could conceivably be released from prison either on parole or after completion of his sentence, but would likely never be released from a mental hospital. Szasz pointed out that the goal of the mental hospital should be the rehabilitation of the patient. It seemed as if Ellis were suggesting the use of the institution as a form of permanent imprisonment. Szasz stated that doctors should not be jailers and pointed to the similarities between the use of psychology as jailer in contemporary society and organized religion as jailer during the inquisition. Both incarcerated those who (1) did not "believe" and (2) refused to acquiesce to the demand to refute their beliefs.

Ellis was asked how he would diagnose and treat David Berkowitz, to which he replied that the "Son of Sam" was a paranoid schizophrenic who was born with the disease. Ellis felt that Berkowitz would be a "tough customer" in therapy, but believed that he could possibly be talked into changing his philosophy of life. Szasz rejected the language of the discussion, feeling the matter to be one of criminal law, not psychology. For Szasz, the point is that doctors should not be charged with controlling social misbehavior. "Healers should never harm other humans," said Szasz, and should never deprive people of their liberties. In Ellis' scheme, the apparent contradiction is that while he was acknowledging the possibility of a cure for Berkowitz, he was also saying that there was less chance of him being released from a mental hospital than from a prison.

The subject of suicide was a topic briefly raised in this debate. Szasz called suicide "the most fundamental human right" and felt that it was absurd to have suicide labeled a criminal act. Ellis and Szasz both agreed that it is preferable for people to be shown that their lives may not have to end yet, but Ellis went on to say that most people should be talked out of suicide. Ellis did say, however, that a person who has thought it through thoroughly and still wishes to end his or her life should be so entitled.

Several questions surrounding the relative merits of specific types of therapies were raised during this debate, including questions on Freudian Psychoanalysis, Primal Scream, and Rational-Emotive Therapy. Albert Ellis was highly critical of both Primal Scream and Freudian therapy, calling the former "screwed up," and the latter "asinine." Ellis explained that while he was trained in Freudian techniques, he now felt that any professional who believed in it was either stupid or seriously ill themselves. Szasz rejected the notion of criticizing forms of therapy since for him there is no such thing as organized psychotherapy. In his existential context, Szasz feels that therapies are "religions," and any form is perfectly fine as long as it is engaged in by consenting adults. He stated quite clearly that psychologists should refrain from judging forms of therapy, and said that in the case of Primal Scream therapy, "if they want to scream, let them," which drew a sustained laugh from the audience.

A great deal of the question and answer period was spent discussing the role of psychiatry in society and the limits of psychological theorizing. Ellis felt that Szasz was being overly idealistic and failed to accept that there are evils on both sides of the issues which they were discussing. Ellis stated his belief that mental illness, while not a perfect term, is nevertheless a description which is effective in identifying degrees of abnormality. Szasz agreed that mental illness is a question of degree, but of degree to which an individual is believed to be in variance with the psychologists' points of view. Szasz said "if your behavior upsets you, you're neurotic; if you upset others, you're psychotic."

Szasz feels that the language of the psychiatric profession does not allow for mental health. He said during this debate that "no one is ever well in the psychiatric language." He believes that the language is both "scientistic" and "positivistic," and is a "dehumanization of those being judged by those judging." The examples Szasz used were in his description of values ("other people have biases, we have values") and in his opinion of schizophrenics being "boundlessly conceited," which offends psychiatrists, who also are. While this latter comment was somewhat "tongue-in-cheek," it does show how Szasz feels that the language of psychiatry is based in loaded terminology.

The language of psychiatry is also of primary importance to the issue of involuntary mental hospitalization. Szasz argued during this debate that while people cannot be locked up for having a physical illness, they can for having a so-called mental illness. Ellis raised the issue of quarantining of certain people with highly infectious diseases, to which Szasz pointed out that quarantines have only been used when not enough was known about a disease, and that such quarantines were designed to protect other people, not the diseased person. Szasz argued that the protection of society is a criminal justice issue, not a psychiatric one, and thus the position of locking people up in order to protect them from themselves is completely inconsistent with their fundamental human rights. Involuntary hospitalization, if justified on the grounds of protecting society from the individual, effectively becomes an alternative method of punitive incarceration, but one devoid of many fundamental civil rights.

Szasz described involuntary mental hospitalization as a "crime against humanity" in his most scathing attack of the evening's debate. He went on to say that scientific methods of hypothesis and proof are nothing more than a "deceitful game" when used by psychiatrists to incarcerate people or to pass judgment on them. This description applies also to the use of drug therapy in the treatment of mental patients. Drug therapy, for Szasz, "is a racket of infinite proportion." Ellis agreed that drugs should not be thought of as cures, but rather as symptom regulators. Szasz, in arguing that "involuntary mental hospitalization is a criminal act," included involuntary drug treatments among his supporting reasons for this belief, believing it to be a crime to administer drugs to people against their will.

For Dr. Szasz, the question of releasing all mental patients from involuntary incarceration is one that needs to be refined. He stated that he would remove the compulsion for people to be in a mental hospital, much as the *compulsion* to be kept in slavery was repealed in the 1860s. People could remain in mental hospitals if they chose, in Szasz's framework, for to compel them to leave is as much a violation of their civil rights as keeping them involuntarily. The issue of releasing all mental patients is also complicated by the fact that many criminals are remanded to institutions. A blanket release of all involuntary mental patients would be conceivable if the institutions had not been used as an alternative form of imprisonment, but in view of the reality of the situation, the "criminals" would need either to be imprisoned if convicted, or tried if not having been so previously.

Throughout the debate, Dr. Ellis continued to support the position that the differences between himself and Dr. Szasz were as much value judgments as are those which Szasz accuses the field of psychiatry having. Ellis believes that the description of mental illness as a myth is a value judgment in itself, to which Szasz disagrees. Szasz feels that there are fundamental distinctions between disorders and deviance that go beyond value judgments. For Szasz, disorders are identifiable characteristics within the individual, while deviances are those characteristics or actions identified through a set of socially determined rules of behavior. Mental illness is a myth in this framework and certainly is not a value judgment of individual behavior.

The issue of labels applied to behavior has been addressed throughout this discourse. This issue was also raised in the context of the removal of homosexuality as a disease from the DSM Manual of Psychiatric Disorders. Szasz contended that in medicine, diagnoses of illnesses do change, but only when new information compels that change. Szasz stated that there is no newly discovered information about homosexuality that should cause a reclassification of it. While he believes that the DSM is essentially a fictional work, his point is that the American Psychiatric Association changed their stance on homosexuality as a result of politics. Voting as a means of de-classifying an illness is a purely "political act," according to Szasz, and violates the principles of science. Homosexuality is what it was before the APA got involved in calling it a disease or not, and has not changed. This, for Szasz, is an excellent example of how psychiatry can cause great harm by labeling individuals and casting a shadow over their lives.

On the issues of racism and sexism, Dr. Szasz once again takes the psychiatric profession to task. Citing historical references dating to the time of legalized slavery in the United States, Szasz pointed to descriptions of disorders which explained such behaviors as slaves escaping, or not doing their chores up to standard. These explanations, couched in the framework of the medical model, attached disease or disorder labels to behaviors that clearly have no rational reason to be labeled as such. This type of selectivity in choosing what are or are not disorders has also been applied to women over the years. In the late 1800s, a law was still on the books in Jackson, Illinois which allowed for the detainment of women in a mental hospital at the request of their husbands, *whether or not* any particular disorder was diagnosed. Szasz used these examples to show how psychiatry has been invading our society since its very inception, and urged the APA to issue a blanket apology for these positions.

Szasz believes strongly that minorities and lower economic classes of our society are "disproportionately treated harshly by the psychiatric profession". He stated that treatments such as electro-shock, chemotherapy, and other more harsh treatments are often chosen over talk therapies with lower socio-economic classes of people. It was at this point during the debate that Szasz referred to psychiatrists as "evil," "bastards," and "money-grubbing." Dr. Ellis took offense to this, accusing Szasz of being guilty of as much labeling and stereotyping as he accused the psychiatric profession of being. Szasz's response was to quote Sartre, saying "people are the sum total of their actions," feeling that psychiatrists are basically guilty of often-times exhibiting behaviors that fit the labels. I do not believe Szasz meant to be taken completely seriously in these condemning statements, but was instead attempting to incite his audience to take action against the injustices sometimes committed by the psychiatric profession.

Where do we go from here?

The issues raised and the scope of the debate between Dr. Ellis and Dr. Szasz are encompassing of many of the current concerns in the mental health field. Psychologists, psychiatrists, and other mental health professionals need to be aware of the controversies in the field, such as whether or not we should incarcerate some mental patients against their will, and should be actively seeking improvements to current inadequacies. This debate also served to exemplify how much divergence of opinion there is in the mental health field today. The point to be emphasized here is that thoughtful, reasonable people sometimes disagree—there are many ways to approach difficult issues, but to avoid them or deny their existence accomplishes nothing productive. This debate showed the way for critical analysis and discussion of many difficult issues and, if nothing else, has stimulated some of us who either attended the discussion or have heard the recording to pursue these issues with a mind open to change and the discovery of new solutions to long-existing problems.

Reference

Szasz, Thomas S. & Ellis, Albert (Speakers). (1997) *Mental Illness: Fact or Myth* [Cassette Tape]. Baldwin, N.Y.: W.E. Simon.

Suggestions for Further Reading/Information

American Psychiatric Association. (1994). *Diagnostic and Statistical Manual of Mental Disorders* (4th ed.). Washington, D.C.: Author

The Barbara Simpson Program. Guest Dr. E. Fuller Torrey. KGO Radio (San Francisco, CA) 2 Nov. 1988.

Bellah, Robert N. (1978). Religious Studies as "New Religion." In a G. Baker & J. Needleman (Eds.), *Understanding the New Religions* (p.106-112). New York: Seabury Press.

Blueler, E. (1950). *Dementia Praecox, or the Group of Schizophrenias*, trans. Joseph Zinkin (International University Press; New York).

Coleman, Lee (1985); Using Psychiatry to Fight 'Cults': Three Case Histories." In a Broch K. Kilborne (Ed.), *Scientific Research and New Religions: Divergent Perspectives; vol. 2, Part 2* (p.40-56). San Francisco, CA: Pacific division, American Association for the Advancement of Science.

Erikson, Erik H. (1964). *Insight and Responsibility.* Toronto, CA: George J. McLeod Limited.

Goleman, David. (1978). The Impact of the New Religions on Psychology. In a G. Baker & J Needleman (Eds.), *Understanding the New Religions* (p. 113-121). New York: Seabury Press.

Gove, Philip Babcock (Ed. In Chief). (1976). *Websters's Third International Dictionary.* Springfield, MA: G. & C. Miriam Company, p. 1100.

Hill, Colin (Prod.) "Doctor Death." Stone Phillips (Reporter). *20/20*. ABC Television. September 1988.

Hollingshead, August B. (1973). Mental Illness: The Rights of the Individual Versus Community Needs. In a Grant H. Morris (Ed.), *The Mentally Ill and the Right to Treatment* (78-94). Springfield, IL: Thomas.

Hombs, Mary Ellen & Snyder, Mitch. (1983) *Homelessness in America: A Forced March to Nowhere*. Washington, D.C.: Community For Creative Nonviolence.

Katz, Jay. (1969). The Right to Treatment—An Enchanting Legal Fiction? *University of Chicago Law Review*. 36. 755-263.

Koch, Sigmund. (1981). The Nature and Limits of Psychological Knowledge. *American Psychologist*. 36. (3), 257-269.

Kolb, L.C. (1968). *Noyes Modern Clinical Psychiatry*, 7th Ed. Saunders: Philadelphia.

Kutner, Luis. (1962). The Illusion of Due Process in Commitment Proceedings. *Northwestern University Law Review*. 57, 383-399.

Marschall, Patricia H. (1973). A Critique of the "Right To Treatment" Approach. In a Grant H. Morris (Ed.) *The Mentally Ill and the Right To Treatment* (37-62). Springfield, IL: Thomas.

Roszak, Theodore. (1978) Ethics, Ecstasy, and the Study of New Religions. In a G. Baker & J. Needleman (Eds.), *Understanding the New Religions* (pp. 49-62). New York: Seabury Press.

Savodnik, Irwin. (1985). [Review of *Ceremonial Chemistry*]. *The Psychiatric Times*, June 1985, 16-17.

Scheff, T. (1966) *Being Mentally Ill*. Aldine: Chicago.

Schoenfeld, C.G. (1976). An Analysis of the Views of Thomas Szasz. *Journal of Psychiatry and Law.* 4, 245-263.

Sobel, Dava. (1987). Raskilvikov Could Cop a Plea [*Review of Insanity: The Idea and Its Consequences*]. *The New York Times Book Review*, March 15, 22.

Szasz, Thomas. (1970). Justice in the Therapeutic State. In The Administration of Justice in America: The 1968-69 E. Paul du Pont Lectures on Crime, Delinquency, and Corrections (75-92). Newark, DL: University of Delaware Press.

Szasz, Thomas. (1974). *Ceremonial Chemistry: The Ritual Persecution of Drugs, Addicts, and Pushers.* New York: Doubleday.

Szasz, Thomas, (1975) Medical Metamorphology. *American Psychologist.* 30, 359-861.

Szasz, Thomas S. & Ellis, Albert (Speakers). (1977). *Mental Illness: Fact or Myth* [Cassette Tape]. Baldwin, N.Y.: W.E. Simon.

Szasz, Thomas S. (1977). *Psychiatric Slavery.* New York: The Free Press.

Szasz, Thomas. (1977). *The Theology of Medicine.* Baton Rouge, LA: LSU Press.

Szasz, Thomas (1987). *Insanity—The Idea and Its Consequences.* New York: John Wiley and Sons.

Szasz, Thomas. (1987). Justifying Coercion through Religion and Psychiatry. *Journal of Humanistic Psychology.* 27 (2), 158-177.

Szasz, Thomas. (1988). Homelessness is Not a Disease. *USA Today.* March, pp 28-29.

Vatz, Richard E. & Weinberg, Lee S. (Eds.) (1983). *Thomas Szasz: Primary Values and Major Contentions*. Buffalo, N.Y.: Prometheus Books.

0-595-31272-1

Printed in the United Kingdom
by Lightning Source UK Ltd.
123671UK00002B/304/A